Math Game 3

Math Game 3

ISBN: 981-05-2768-3

Printed in the Republic of Korea.

Distributed by Publishers Group West.

How to contact us

E-mail: feedback@youngjin.com.sg

Address: Youngjin Singapore Pte, Ltd.
70 Anson Road, #22-04, Apex Tower
Singapore 079905

Telephone: +65-6327-1161
Fax: +65-6327-1151

Manager: Suzie Lee
Production Editor: Cris Lee
Copy editor: Elisabeth Beller
Proofreaders: Elisabeth Beller, Rand Miranda

Story: Tori Jung
Art: Haley Chung
Color: Winsorblue

Book Designer: Litmus
Cover Designer: Namu & Litmus

Math Game 3

Escape from the Evil Math King!

5

72

sam

Story | Tori Jung
Art | Haley Chung
Color | Winsorblue

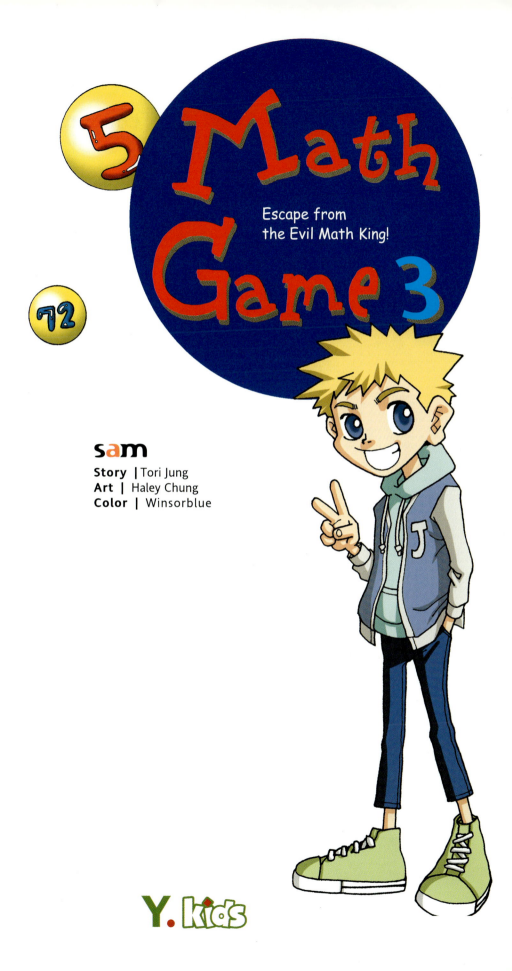

Y. kids

The *Math Game* series is not linked to a specific curriculum for children. It is a supplementary tool to help children learn the principles of mathematics naturally through interesting stories. While enjoying the comics, children will discover interesting and real-life aspects of mathematics. There are no supplemental study pages in the text because the book has been designed in a way that allows children to learn on their own while reading. There is a review section at the end of the book to remind children of what they have learned.

Principles of mathematics are explained thoroughly so that anyone who can read and understand English can understand them. Although this book is intended for third graders or older students, the episodes will be interesting for adults as well.

The storyline is as follows: In *Math Game 1*, children who dislike mathematics speak ill of it. The Evil Math King hears them and is angered. He captures one of the children and then challenges the others to come to Math Land to try to save their friend. The children soon discover the pathway to Math Land, which opens each time they discover a fact of mathematics used in their daily lives. On arriving at Math Land, the children find that they must pass through a number of gates. In *Math Game 2*, as in *Math Game 1*, each gate is guarded by a master of mathematics who gives out problems the children must solve in order to progress. While passing through each gate, the children get more and more interested in mathematics. Do they finally save their friend? You will find the answer to this question in *Math Game 3*.

Leave this book near children. When they open it, they will discover the world of mathematics!

Math Game 3 contains seven episodes that teach about magic squares, proportion and Fibonacci numbers.

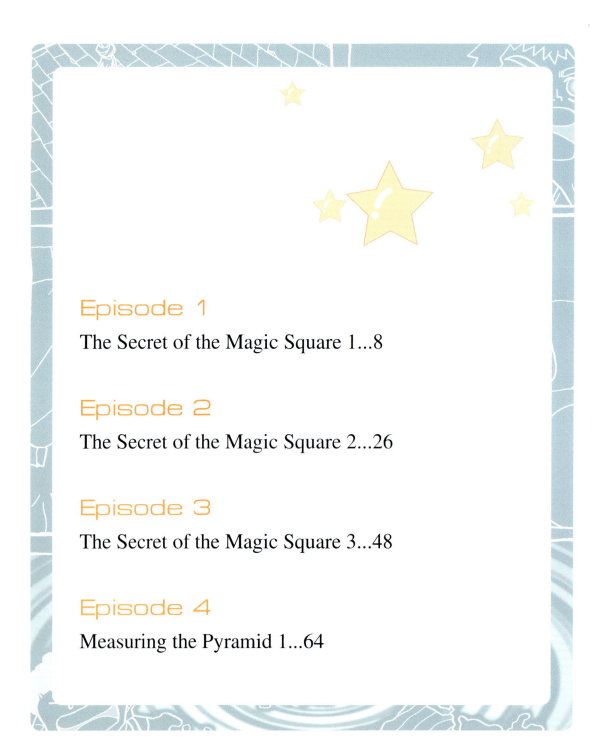

Episode 1

The Secret of the Magic Square 1...8

Episode 2

The Secret of the Magic Square 2...26

Episode 3

The Secret of the Magic Square 3...48

Episode 4

Measuring the Pyramid 1...64

Contents

Episode 5
Measuring the Pyramid 2...94

Episode 6
Proportion...111

Episode 7
The Truth about the Evil Math King...138

Well...everybody done? You want me to start?

Okay. Good. Go ahead.

Every time I call a number, you guys mark that number I called on your grid. The one who is first to get three marked numbers in a straight line going horizontally, vertically, or diagonally yell out "BINGO!"

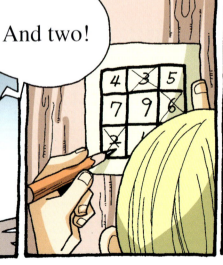

SPLASH

Take a close look. If the small hole over there is a one, that one in the center could be a five, the one in on the left is a three, and the other one on the right is a seven. The top one is a nine.

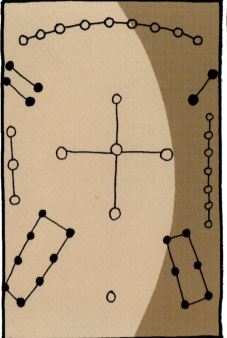

So? What about it?

I guess I see Jimmy's point. In that case, when you look at that diagonally, those on the right side are four and eight. The others on the right side are two and six.

I see, I see... You could see it that way. But what is so strange about that?

Hmm... I guess those numbers are supposed to mean something.

I know! They're going to regret leaving us like this!

Let's get out of here.

Come on guys...

Here I go!

ZEEE
ZEEEET

OWW!!!

I'm the fattest one here so I'm going to die first! Boo hooo!!

What were those numbers??? Arghhh! C'mon! Think! Think, Jimmy!

The number here is definitely four.
The turtle had four dots on its back.

Right. The number there was four.

Well. But, how do I make the sign of "4"? Fingers are "5". Toes are "5". What can I use to make a "4"???

Use your arms and legs!

That's right! I have two arms and two legs, so they will stand for the number "4"!!

Socks!

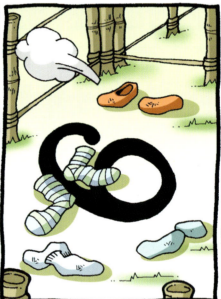

You fools!! We need six, not eight! Not all of us need to throw socks!!

wwwww!!! Whose socks are these?!

ACCCKK!!!

Jimmy!! Jimmy!! Wake up!!!

Wh-what? What are you doing to me?!

Aaack!!

Hey, I'm the one who saved his life.

Ahem! Well, you've got talent. The first magic square is not an easy question. But you still have a long way to go to get home.

Puhahahaha!

The new grid you're locked in is the second magic square.

Another magic square?!!!

Yes. Numbers in this square are arranged according to a certain rule. Your task is to find out the rule.

What rule???

Right... the arrangement is strange.

I know. I think they can't be random numbers, but...

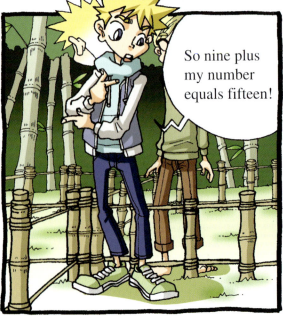

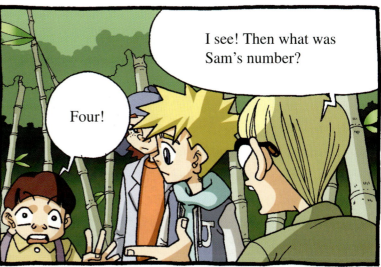

I see! Then what was Sam's number?

Four!

Go ahead. You answer.

No, we can say it together.

Huk!

EPISODE 4
Measuring the Pyramid 1

Wow! It's so high that I can't see the top!

How tall is the building?

No way! How?! You can't fool us again!

Watch me. I'll show you guys how to measure it.

See? This tile is one meter in height, right?

Yes.

Oh no!!
This can't be
happening!!

Guys,
I think
something
is missing!

What?

Wow!
Look at the top!
It's too tall to
see it clearly.

Yeah!
It really is
tall, I wonder
how tall that
building is?

Uhh?
Why does this
conversation
seem so familiar?

That must be the tenth gatekeeper.

It's so obvious now.

I'm just wondering what question he will give us.

I hope the next question will be easier than the others...

You must be surprised and wondering who I am...

You're the tenth gatekeeper!!

How did you know that?

How can't we know that? This is not the first time we've been here.

Right. This is our tenth visit here!

COUGH

COUGH

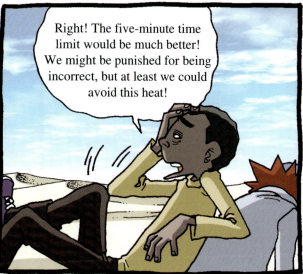

EPISODE 5
Measuring the Pyramid 2

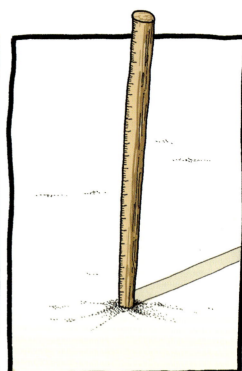

We have no time to discuss this. Let's measure the length of the shadow first.

I got it!

Well done. Using the shadow! What a smart idea!

We got the correct answer. Let me and my friends go back home.

Haha! Why in so much of a hurry? Don't you want to know how it works?

We're terribly thirsty! Just let us go!

Oh no!! I almost forgot!

Here you go.

Wow! This is the tastiest water that I've ever had!

Whewww! This is so good!

Right.
This way of playing the game is really exciting!!

In ancient times, measuring the height of something tall was a headache. So people used the shadow to measure high mountains and tall structures.

And I'm the first person to measure the height of the pyramid using the shadow.

What? Then... are you famous?

Puhahahaha! You already know my reputation!

So what is my name?

I don't know.

Hahaha!

My name is Thales.

Thales!!

In the year 6 BC, the pharaoh ordered me to measure the pyramid of Kufu and I used this method.

At that time, people were so anxious to know what kind of complicated method I used to measure the height of the pyramid.

The real pyramid is just a large version of the shadow pyramid. Same shape, different size. That's the theory that I used to measure the height of the pyramid.

Oh, I see!!

Well, this is the end of the practice session!

What?? Practice???

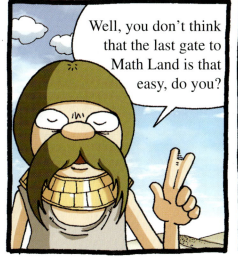

Well, you don't think that the last gate to Math Land is that easy, do you?

Really? Is this the last gate?!

Really?

Yes, it is. This is the last gate!

And if you fail this last question, everything will end up in smoke.

Eh? This is strange. The number of petals is similar. This one has three petals, and that one has five petals... Eight there and thirteen here...

EPISODE 6
Proportion

Look at the shadow. It is longer than the actual height of the pyramid right now.

Wow! It really is!

Now, the length of the shadow and stick are no longer equal. So how do you measure the height of the pyramid now? Measure the height of the pyramid over there.

Again? You want us to measure the height of that other pyramid?

This is the last question to Math Land. This is your last gate!!

MUAHAHAHA!

Why is he doing that??

What a show-off.

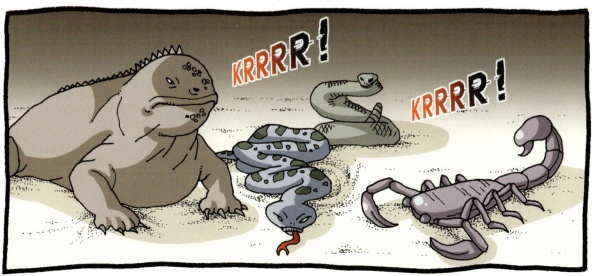

WAAAAHHH!
We're scared!!

Hey guys!
This is the last gate. He wouldn't give us a question that has no answer.
We can do it.
Let's the find answer.

We already know how. The only way to get the answer is to wait.

Right.

If the stick's shadow is twice as long as the stick, then all we have to do is to divide the the length for pyramid's shadow in half...

Right!! And if it's three times longer...

...divide the pyramid's shadow's length in thirds...

We got it!!! Bravo!!

Here! The stick's shadow is now three times longer than the stick!

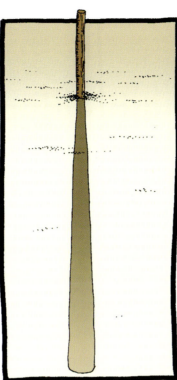

Great! Let's hurry. We need the length of the pyramid's shadow!!

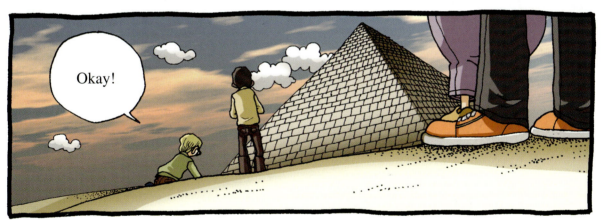

Okay!

So... 2,255, 2,256...

Soon the Evil Math King will arrive. Then he will test you for the last time...

What? What kind of last test!!!!?

...to see if you are passing all of these gates because of your good luck or your true abilities!

Only when you pass his test, can you go home safely with Alice.

Grrrr... What kind of promise is that?

It's not what we were promised at the beginning! We were told "ten gates"! Ten!!

Are you the kids who passed through all of the gates of Math Land!?!

Can't you hear what I'm saying?! Answer my question!!!

What are you doing?!!! Answer the King's question!

Well...

...yes, we are...

Since I haven't seen it with my own eyes, I can't believe it. But if you answer my question now, I will believe you!

But that's not fair! Passing ten gates was what you promised!

Eh?

So?? Aha!!
I knew it!
That's it!!

Okay,
give us the question.

Muhahaha!
Good.

Here,
in this bottle
is a creature
that is dividing
in half to form
a new creature
every second.

It takes sixty
seconds for the
dividing creatures to
fill this bottle.

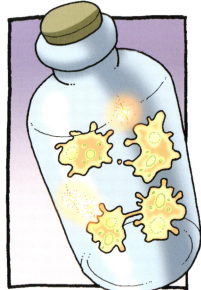

Then just give him the answer and rescue Alice right away!

EPISODE 7
The Truth about the Evil Math King

Wait! Why are you in such a hurry? This question is too simple for a final question.

But this is about multiplying. This is not a nonsense quiz.

Right. Why hesitate? Let's get Alice back right now!

We got it!

Go ahead! Answer!

Not much time left. Are you going to answer or not?!!

Hey, Jimmy. Listen.

Okay.

One of these animals in the bottle divides to make two animals every one second. It takes sixty seconds for them to fill the one bottle. How long will it take to fill both bottles?

Isn't it obvious? Just double...

Wait! That's the Evil Math King of Math Land. I can't believe that he'd give us such an easy question!

Jimmy!
He's got Alice
with him too!!

What?
Alice??

Let's just answer
him and take
Alice back!

Uhmm...
uhhh...

This is not
going to work!
Jimmy can't
concentrate whenever
he hears
about Alice.

Then let's calm
down and think
carefully. That
creature doubles
every second.

Yes...
Then how long will it
take for the one
bottle to become
two bottles???

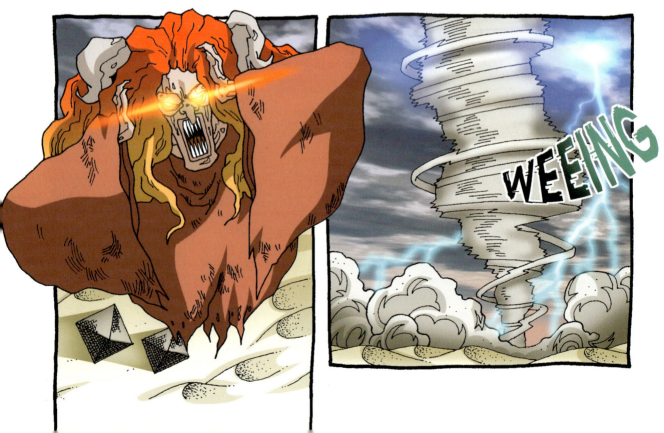

WEEING

The Evil Math King is in a rage! Please, we beg you to calm down, my lord!!

Alice!!!

No!! The Evil Math King tricked us!! That's a doll, not Alice!

Hurry! Let's go find her!

Let's check this way first! That's where the Evil Math King was running.

Right!

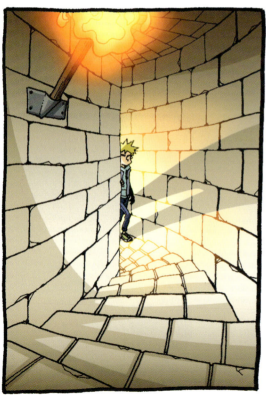

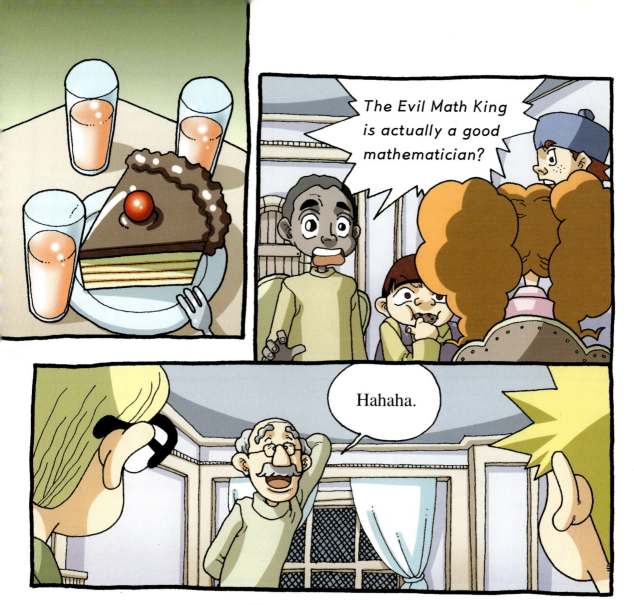

The Evil Math King is actually a good mathematician?

Hahaha.

Yes. He was sorry to see us under so much pressure because of math. So he planned it all.

He gave me math lessons here. I never knew that math could be this interesting and easy.

What is Magic Square?

A Magic Square is a square array of numbers consisting of distinct positive integers that are arranged so the sum of the numbers in any horizontal, vertical or main diagonal line is always the same number.

The origin of the Magic Square is not known though it has been attributed to China's King Wu of the early Ha dynasty. It is said that the idea occurred to the king when he spotted a turtle with odd markings while working on a stream to set it up for flood control.

Later, Arab traders spread word of the Magic Square across the rest of Asia and beyond.

In the 16th century, the German artist Durer used a Magic Square as a background in his work called "Melancholia" and this piece of art helped spread the Magic Square around Europe during that era.

Thales, the first mathematician to measure the height of the pyramids

Measuring the height of mountains and tall structures wasn't easy in ancient times and any person who could measure up was looked up at with great respect.

In the 6th century BC, Thales from Miletos was given the task of measuring the height of the pyramid for Kufu, a pharaoh of that time.

Thales waited for a cloudless day and set out on his task, armed with only a stick. He stuck the stick in the ground and waited until the height of the stick's shadow was equal to the length of the stick.

He then ordered some workers to measure the length of the pyramid's shadow.

Fibonacci Numbers

Fibonacci was an Italian mathematician in the 12th century.

One day, he came up with an interesting math question: If a pair of rabbits on a farm begin to reproduce two months after their own birth, then how many pairs of rabbits can be produced from that pair in one year if each pair has a new pair every month and none die?

He reasoned: After one month, there is a pair of rabbits. After two months, there are two pairs since the first pair had another pair. After three months, there are three pairs since the first pair had another pair but the second pair was still too young to have any rabbits.

After fours months, he wrote, there would be five pairs since the first pair and the second pair would both have a pair and so on until the year was up.

The resulting sequence of numbers (1, 2, 3, 5, 8, 13, 21, 34, 55, 89 ...) are now called Fibonacci numbers after the Italian theorist.

The definition of it is that each Fibonacci number is obtained by adding the two previous Fibonacci numbers together.

This theory is proved accurate in nature as many flowers follow this theory. Lily and iris, for example, have three petals. Acris and wild rose have petals. Larkspur has 8, cineraria has 13, chicory has 21, Asian plainrain has 34 and aster has either 55 or 80 petals.

The connection between the number of petals and Fibonacci numbers is a matter of efficiency for petals to protect its pistil and stamen during growth and plant reproduction.